Lucky Duck

by Teddy Slater
illustrated by Kellie Lewis

SCHOLASTIC INC.

New York • Toronto • London • Auckland • Sydney
Mexico City • New Delhi • Hong Kong • Buenos Aires

No part of this publication may be reproduced, stored in a retrieval system, or transmitted in any form or by any means, electronic, mechanical, photocopying, recording, or otherwise, without written permission of the publisher. For information regarding permission, write to Scholastic Inc., Attention: Permissions Department, 557 Broadway, New York, NY 10012.

Designed by Maria Lilja
ISBN-13: 978-0-439-88456-3 • ISBN-10: 0-439-88456-X
Copyright © 2006 by Scholastic Inc.
All rights reserved. Printed in the U.S.A.

First printing, September 2006

12 11 10 9 8 7 6 5 4 3 2 1   6 7 8 9 10 11/0

Phonics Fact

The letter *u* is a vowel. A vowel can make a short sound. The short-*u* sound is found in words such as **duck, up**, and **luck**. What other short-*u* words can you find in this story? Look at the pictures, too!

One **sunny Sunday, Duck** woke **up** in **such** a great mood. He had a **hunch** this would be his **lucky** day.

Phonics Fact

Sometimes the short-*u* sound comes in the second syllable of a word, such as in sy**rup**.

Duck rushed downstairs. He was **hungry** for **plum** pancakes with plenty of **butter** and **syrup**.

Duck opened the **cupboard**. **Uh-oh**! No **plums**.

So **Duck jumped** in his **truck** and headed to
Gus's Store to get some **plums**. **But** the **truck**
hit a **bump** and would not **budge**.

When **Duck** got out of his **truck—yuck**!
He stepped in a big **puddle** of **mud**.

"I will **just** have to walk," said **Duck**. **But** along
the way, he got **stuck** in **bubble gum**. Ugh!

Still, **Duck trudged** on. That is, **until** he got
stung on the **thumb** by a **bumblebee**.
What an **ugly lump**!

By the time **Duck** got to **Gus's** Store, his **tummy** was **rumbling**. He was very **hungry**, **plus** very **grumpy**.

Duck had never felt less **lucky**. Then, **uh-oh**!
He dropped his **plums**.

But suddenly... **Duck** heard a **drum** roll.
Then **Gus** said, "Congratulations! You are the
one **hundredth customer** of the **summer**."

Gus gave **Duck** a **hug** and a **coupon** for a free
brunch at the **Snug** Diner on **Huff** Street.

Duck rushed off to the Snug Diner and placed his order: a stack of **plum** pancakes with plenty of **butter** and **syrup**.

Yum! It was **just** what he wanted. Oh, what a **lucky duck**!

Short-u Riddles

Listen to the riddles. Then match each riddle
with the right short-*u* word from the box.

> **Word Box**
>
> yum   duck   snug   luck   up
> jump   plum   Sunday   butter   summer

1. This animal says, "Quack, quack."

2. You put this on toast or popcorn.

3. This is the day after Saturday.

4. It is the opposite of *down*.

5. This word rhymes with *rug*.

6. A four-leaf clover brings this.

7. It means almost the same thing as *leap*.

8. This is the season after spring.

9. You say this when something is delicious.

10. This purple fruit is bigger than a grape.

Short-u Cheer

Hooray for short *u*, the best sound around!

Let's holler short-*u* words all over town!

There's **mug** and **sun** and **lunch** and **up**.

There's **gum** and **fun** and **luck** and **cup**.

There's **bug** and **hut** and **hum** and **rug**.

There's **lump** and **run** and **chum** and **hug**.

Short *u*, short *u*, give a great cheer,

For the **luckiest** sound you ever will hear!

short u

Make a list of other short-*u* words. Then use them in your cheer.